394.2
~~9804268~~
PAT
Chr

Patterson, Lillie

Christmas feasts
and festivals

820204

A HOLIDAY BOOK

Christmas
Feasts and Festivals

BY LILLIE PATTERSON

ILLUSTRATED BY CLIFF SCHULE

GARRARD PUBLISHING COMPANY
CHAMPAIGN, ILLINOIS

For Grandmother Cornelia
who taught me to love words

Holiday books are edited under
the educational supervision of

Charles E. Johnson, Ed.D.
Professor of Education
University of Georgia

The author and publisher acknowledge with thanks permission received to reprint the following poems in this book.
The Viking Press, Inc. for "Words from an Old Spanish Carol" from *The Long Christmas* by Ruth Sawyer. Copyright 1941 by Ruth Sawyer. J. M. Dent & Sons Ltd. (London) for "Polish Lullaby" from *A Christmas Book*.

Contents

1. The Wonder of Christmas

Christmas is coming!

Bells ring out the news. Voices carol over the frosty air: "Joy! Joy! Joy!"

The magical spell of excitement spreads through schools, stores, and streets. Colorful decorations turn the midwinter world into a wonderland of beauty.

Homes now hum with holiday hustle and bustle. Families begin making and hanging wreaths and holiday calendars. How many days till Christmas? Twenty, ten, five, one. Then comes the most joyful cry of the year: "Merry Christmas to you!"

The first Christmas came nearly 2,000 years ago. It brought the same sense of excitement and expectation, the same tidings of great joy. These verses from the Bible tell the wonderful story:

And there were in the same country
Shepherds abiding in the field,
Keeping watch over their flock by night.
And, lo, the angel of the Lord
    came upon them;
And the glory of the Lord
    shone round about them;
And they were sore afraid.
And the angel said unto them, "Fear not!

For, behold, I bring you good tidings
    of great joy,
Which shall be to all people.
For unto you is born this day
    in the city of David
A Saviour, which is Christ the Lord.
And this shall be a sign unto you:
Ye shall find the babe wrapped
    in swaddling clothes,
Lying in a manger."
And suddenly there was with the angel
A multitude of the heavenly host
Praising God, and saying,
"Glory to God in the highest,
And on earth peace,
Good will toward men."

Jesus, the Christ Child, was born that night. Christ's lessons of love, peace and brotherhood changed the lives of men and nations. The people who followed Christ's teachings became known as Christians.

No one recorded the date when Jesus was born. Since early Christians honored their leaders' death days rather than their birthdays, this did not matter at first. When later Christians wished to celebrate Christ's birthday, they had to choose a date. They chose December 25. The story of why this date was chosen goes back to very ancient times.

2. Long Before Christmas

Cold, bleak winters were times of sadness to ancient people. Most of them worshiped the sun. Winter ended the splendor of the sun god's rule, they believed. The evil powers of darkness took over, trying to kill all living things.

Days grew shorter and nights longer. People feared that the sun god might never return. Late December brought a turning point, however. Days grew longer. Sunlight glowed stronger. "The sun god has begun his journey back to us," people cried.

They held gay festivals to welcome his return. They lighted candles and bonfires to make the sun stronger and drive winter away.

Countries of the Roman Empire had a special holiday on December 25, called the "Birthday of the Sun." The holiday came at the end of a week-long festival called Saturnalia. It honored Saturn, the Roman god of seed-time and plenty.

During Saturnalia no one worked except cooks and bakers. "All schools, courts, and businesses shall close," the Roman rulers ordered. "Soldiers must lay down their weapons. All men shall be equal—slave and free, rich and poor, one with another."

Buildings were decorated with evergreens, symbols of lasting sunlight. Friends exchanged wreaths made of laurel leaves, the Roman symbol of victory and honor. Men, women, and children paraded in fancy costumes. Sometimes they carried small trees trimmed with candles to welcome the sun's return.

Saturnalia lasted from December 17–24. It was a time of singing, feasting, and general merrymaking. On December 25, ceremonies with lighted candles and lamps honored the sun god.

The Kalends of January, the Romans' New Year festival, began a few days later. It lasted from January first to about January third.

Roman officials were sworn into office. Friends exchanged gifts and good wishes for the coming year. Celebrations for Kalends were much like those for Saturnalia. In fact, Saturnalia, the Birthday of the Sun, and Kalends made one continuous festival.

Tribes of people living in Britain and Scandinavia held similar midwinter sun festivals. They called theirs Yule, or *Jol,* from which the word "jolly" comes. They, too, used evergreens in ceremonies and celebrations. They lighted huge Yule logs and feasted on roasted boars. These wild hogs were then plentiful in northern Europe.

The pagan midwinter festivals remained popular centuries after Christ was born. Meanwhile, the Christian religion continued to grow stronger. Many Christians began to observe Christ's birthday. Since no one knew His birthdate, some people celebrated in spring, others in winter.

Finally, Church leaders in Rome adopted

December 25 as Christ's birthday. This was in the fourth century, A.D., over 300 years after Christ was born.

December 25 was a wise choice. The date was already a holiday. Churchmen hoped that people would forget their pagan customs, and celebrate Christ's birthday instead.

Early Christian holidays were called feast days. December 25 became the Feast of the Nativity. The word "Nativity" comes from the Latin *Natalis,* meaning birthday. Several names for Christ's birthday came from this word—the Italian *Natale,* the Spanish *Navidad,* the French *Noël.*

A special church service called a Mass was celebrated to honor the Nativity. In England, the day became known as Christ's Mass, later shortened to Christmas. The Scandinavian name for Christmas is *Jul,* or Yule. Germans call the season *Weihnachten,* the Holy Nights.

3. The Twelve Days of Christmas

The first Christmas celebrations were solemn and holy. There were no gay carols or Christmas decorations. Even the songs were solemn, and sung in Latin.

Church leaders made the four-week period before Christmas a sacred season. This was a time to pray and prepare for the coming of the holy festival. They called it "Advent," which means coming.

In the sixth century, the twelve days from December 25 to January 6 were set aside to observe Christmas. January 6,

14

called Epiphany, is a feast day older than the celebration of Christmas. It honors the visit of the Wise Men to the Christ Child. "Epiphany" comes from the Greek word for appearance.

The observance of Christmas spread rapidly between the years 600 and 1100. Religious teachers took Christianity to pagan tribes all over Europe. These pagans were willing to give up their old gods, but they were not willing to give up their folk customs. They wanted to keep on holding merry festivals.

Churchmen finally understood how much these customs meant to the people. So they let the people keep them. Gradually the customs from Saturnalia, Kalends, and Yule became a part of Christmas, and took on new Christian meanings.

During the Middle Ages, Christmastime became the merriest season of the year. People celebrated in homes, streets, and churches. Many of the Christmas traditions, songs, and legends sprang up during the years between 1100 and 1500.

The Twelve Days of Christmas became a time of continuous rejoicing. Each town or village appointed a man to lead all the entertainment. This "Lord of Misrule" had a group of helpers called mummers and jesters. Mummers, or masqueraders, acted in pantomimes or short plays. Jesters decked themselves in bright colors and tied tiny bells to their legs. They clowned, capered, and told jokes.

Kings and noblemen lived in castles and great houses. They held grand feasts and open houses throughout the season. Each castle, great house, inn, or college hired its own Lord of Misrule. Traveling singers and poets also helped to entertain.

The poor peasants made Christmas their favorite holiday. They worked hard all year with little time out for fun. They could forget their work and hardships during the Twelve Days. A Lord of Misrule led them in noisy street parading, dancing, and masquerading. There were pipers piping, drums beating, and bells jingling.

Twelfth Night brought the holiday season to a close. Most families had a Twelfth Night cake to honor the Three Kings. A bean was baked into the batter. The person who found the bean in his slice of cake was made "King of the Bean." His word was law for Twelfth Night. If a girl found the bean, she could choose the king.

17

Games were popular at Twelfth Night parties. In one game, the leader spoke the twelve verses of a poem. The other players repeated them. The verses told of the gifts to match the Twelve Days of Christmas. Anyone who failed to name the gifts in the right order had to pay a forfeit. One version came down as a favorite carol.

On the first day of Christmas
My true love sent to me
A partridge in a pear tree.
— two turtle doves
— three French hens
— four calling birds
— five gold rings
— six geese a-laying
— seven swans a-swimming
— eight maids a-milking
— nine drummers drumming
— ten pipers piping
— eleven dancers dancing
— twelve lords a-leaping.

—Old English Carol

4. The Christmas Feast

Delicious smells of Christmas cooking filled the kitchens of medieval castles and great houses. Steaming cauldrons hung over wide fireplaces. Roasting meats sizzled on turning spits.

At noon on Christmas Day, the knights and ladies marched to the dining hall. Trumpets blew. Jesters capered in, followed by minstrels and the Lord of Misrule. Just behind them marched the cook, holding

high a large platter. On it lay a roasted
boar's head, decorated with sprigs of bay
and rosemary. An apple, orange, or lemon
lay in its mouth. Minstrels led the guests
in singing the "Boar's Head Carol."

> The boar's head in hand bring I,
> Bedecked with bays and rosemary;
> I pray you all sing merrily . . .

A lady at the feast was given the honor
of bringing in a second platter. This held

a peacock. The bird had been skinned, baked, and sewn back into its brilliant feathers. Knights touched the bird and made the "Peacock Vow." Each knight promised to perform a brave deed during the coming year.

Peacocks were sometimes baked into pies. The head stuck out from one end of the pan, and the tail from the other.

Swan was another favorite meat. Five swans were served for Christmas Day, three for New Year's Day, and four for Epiphany.

Many kinds of birds were always baked for Christmas dinners. So were several kinds of fish.

Christmas pies formed the main part of the feasts. Cooks chopped up a hodge-podge of meats to make these enormous pies. Some were baked in an oblong shape to represent the manger. A tiny figure of the Holy Babe stood atop the steaming crust. Christmas pies contained flour, butter, spices, eggs, geese, pigeons, partridges, blackbirds, beef, mutton, and other meats. One famous pie weighed over 100 pounds! Christmas pies later changed into modern mince-meat pies.

The plum porridge, or plum pudding, was a favorite dish, especially in England. Dried plums were used in the days before raisins. Legend tells how the first pudding was made.

Once an English King and his hunting party became lost in a storm. They could

not return home for Christmas. The King's
cook decided to make a feast out of the
foods they had. He mixed deer meat, flour,
plums, apples, sugar, eggs, brandy, and
spices all together. The sticky mixture was
boiled in a bag. Out came the first plum
pudding!

There were many superstitions about
Christmas puddings and pies. If you failed
to eat some, you would lose a friend. If
you ate some on each of the Twelve Days,

you had good luck for twelve months. If you made a wish on the first mouthful, your wish would come true.

Wassail, a favorite Christmas drink, was made from ale, sugar, spices, eggs, cream, and ginger. It was served in a bowl with roasted apples bobbing on top. "Wassail" comes from the German phrase *Was Haile,* meaning "To your health!" or "Good wishes!" People cried "Wassail" to each other as they sipped the drink.

There were grand feasts, not only on Christmas, but on each of the Twelve Days. Poor peasants came each day to eat some of the leftover food. Sometimes they were given special banquets. In 1248, King Henry III of England filled Westminster Hall with poor people. He feasted them for a whole week. Christmas became a season for sharing with those in need.

5.   The Lights of Christmas

When they saw the star,
They rejoiced with exceeding great joy.
—*The Gospel According to St. Matthew*

A star over Bethlehem guided the Wise
Men to the Christ Child in the manger.
The five-pointed star remained a symbol of
Christmas. It holds a place of honor in
decorations, often atop Christmas trees.

The Yule log gave light at Christmas during medieval days. The humblest hut had one. Bringing in the Yule log was an exciting event. Families cut the biggest log their fireplace could hold. On Christmas Eve the log was dragged home amid much singing and cheering.

Everyone in the household tugged on the ropes as the log was dragged indoors.

Sometimes each person sat on the log, sang a song, and kissed it. Sometimes the father prayed and poured wine or grain upon it. This was all done to bring good luck.

A shout of joy rang out when the giant log was placed in the fireplace. Children danced about gaily as the flames sprang up. Yule logs were burned to honor the Nativity. They were also burned to bring peace, safety, and good fortune to homes. A piece of the burnt wood was saved to light the Yule fire another year.

Candles have been used in many religious festivals since pagan times. Christians made the burning candle a symbol of Christ, "The Light of the World."

Children in medieval days helped their mothers make huge Christmas candles, and decorated them with evergreens. These tall, thick candles were lit on Christmas Eve, and on each of the Twelve Nights. They were believed to shed special blessings.

Smaller candles shone from windows of homes. An Irish legend says why. Every Christmas, the story goes, the Christ Child visits homes. Sometimes He sends a stranger instead. Nobody knows how the stranger will look. It may be a hungry child, a beggar, an old woman. The lighted candle says: Here you are welcomed!

Today, wax candles are still lighted in homes and churches at Christmastime. Many families with fireplaces burn logs.

Electricity now makes it possible for our Christmas lights to shine in many colors—red, green, blue, yellow. Their dazzling beauty reminds us that Christmas is truly a Festival of Lights.

Then be ye glad, good people,
This night of all the year,
And light ye up your candles;
His star is shining near.
—*Old Besançon Noël*

6.   Christmas Greens

Sing hey! Sing hey!
For Christmas Day;
Twine mistletoe and holly,
For friendship glows
In winter snows,
And so let's all be jolly.

—*Author Unknown*

Evergreens held out hope to ancient people that the sun would return. Plants that stayed ever green had some of the sun god's magic, they believed. They hung evergreen branches on windows and doors to keep out witches. They brought them inside as protection against the evils of darkness.

Evergreens soon were made symbols of Christmas joy by Christians. When they gathered evergreens, they said, "We're bringing home Christmas." Wreaths on doors and windows were signs of peace and welcome.

Holly was a favorite. The red of its berries and the green of its glossy leaves became Christmas colors. They blend beautifully with the white of winter's snow. White is also the Church color for Christmas.

Ivy hung beside the holly in homes. There was an old belief that ivy brought good luck to women. Holly brought good luck to men.

Mistletoe was sacred to Scandinavians, and to the Druids of Britain. It was called all-heal, and used to cure sickness. It was also a plant of peace. Enemies who met under the mistletoe had to kiss and make up. Kissing customs may have come from this Norse, or Scandinavian, myth:

Balder the Beautiful was god of light, joy, and poetry. Frigga, his mother, begged all living things to keep Balder safe. She forgot the mistletoe. A sharp dart tipped with mistletoe killed Balder.

Frigga wept until her love brought Balder back to life. Her tears formed the pearl-like mistletoe berries. "This plant must never be used for harm," Frigga ordered. "All who stand beneath the mistletoe must kiss in peace and friendship."

Kissing boughs once hung in the center halls of homes. These were double-hooped wreaths of evergreens, decorated with berries and ribbons. From the center hung sprays of mistletoe. Anyone caught under a kissing bough could be kissed.

There were other popular Christmas greens. The large, shiny leaves of the laurel bush, also called bay, made beautiful wreaths. Laurel was the first plant used by Christians to honor Christ's birthday.

Rosemary, a symbol of remembrance, decorated homes and flavored foods. This delicate herb has a nice smell. Rosemary branches were spread over floors during medieval celebrations. When merry-makers danced upon them, the air became perfumed.

People believed that rosemary helped them to stay young.

Legend tells why rosemary is such a lovely plant. Mary, the Mother of Jesus, washed the Holy Babe's clothes. She spread them on a bush to dry. As a reward, the bush was named rosemary. It bore flowers as blue as Mary's mantle, and leaves as fragrant as perfume.

The rose also honored the Virgin Mary. Another legend tells about the Christmas rose. A shepherd girl longed to follow the shepherds who took gifts to the Christ Child. Alas, she had nothing to give. She knelt on the ground weeping. Suddenly an angel appeared and touched the ground with a staff. Beautiful roses sprang up. The girl hastened to the manger with an armful. The Child smiled upon the blooms, and the rose became the queen of flowers.

All nature rejoiced when Christ was born, according to old legends. Every tree and bush blossomed and bore fruit. People of the Middle Ages liked this idea. They decorated homes with trees and branches. Apples, ribbons, trinkets, and paper roses made them colorful.

Some families used real blossoms. Weeks before Christmas, they brought branches of flowering trees indoors. Sometimes they brought in the whole tree. By Christmas, the branches bloomed, brightening homes like rays of spring sun.

7. The Christmas Creche

And they came with haste,

And found Mary and Joseph,

And the babe lying in a manger.

—*The Gospel According to St. Luke*

The story of the Christmas crèche goes back many centuries. Saint Francis of Assisi, Italy, made it popular. St. Francis spent his life preaching and caring for the poor and sick. He taught people to see beauty in all creatures.

Each year, St. Francis tried to explain the Christmas story to poor country folk. They enjoyed the holiday feasting and merrymaking, but the true meaning of Christmas remained a mystery to most.

One day in 1223, St. Francis thought of a plan. He sent word to the towns and countryside near Assisi: "Come and keep Christmas with me."

On Christmas Eve, St. Francis led the people to a rocky cave near the town of Greccio. Men, women, and children carried candles and torches to light the way. They cried out in wonder when they saw the surprise St. Francis had prepared for them.

There was a manger, filled with fresh hay. Beside the manger stood a live ox and a donkey. Real people took the parts of Mary, Joseph, and the shepherds. In the manger lay a life-sized wax baby.

St. Francis explained the story as he showed it. The poor King born in a stable

had brought the hope of a better life for all. Now the listeners began to realize the beauty of the Christmas message. The cave rang with music as St. Francis led the worshipers in joyful singing.

The next Christmas, these people set up their own manger scenes. The custom quickly spread through Italy, and then to other parts of Europe. It helped to make Christmas more popular among poor people and country folk.

Italians called the manger scene *presepe,* their word for stable. The French called it *crèche,* or cradle. Germans called it *Krippe,* or crib. Spanish nations called it *nacimiento,* meaning Nativity scene.

The first crèches or nativity scenes were very simple. Many used live animals and people. As the years passed, these figures were made from wood, clay, wax, or other materials. Crèches were set up in streets, churches, homes, and stores.

Animals were always placed in these scenes. Legends say that animals, too, traveled to Bethlehem to worship the Christ Child. At midnight, they had the gift of speech.

Shall I tell you who will come
      to Bethlehem on Christmas Morn,
Who will kneel them gently down
      before the Lord, new-born?

One small fish from the river,
      with scales of red, red gold,
One wild bee from the heather,
      one gray lamb from the fold,
One ox from the high pasture,
      one black bull from the herd,
One goatling from the far hills,
      one white, white bird.

And many children, God give them grace,
bringing tall candles to light Mary's face.

—*"Words from an Old Spanish Carol"*
Translated by Ruth Sawyer

8. The Voices of Christmas

What sweeter music can we bring,
Than a Carol, for to sing
The Birth of this our heavenly King?
Awake the Voice! Awake the String!
—*Robert Herrick*

"Tell of your Christmas joy in songs!" St. Francis taught his people. He is called "The Father of the Christmas carol."

St. Francis founded a religious order called Franciscans. These priests carried the custom of carol singing across Europe.

They wrote many lovely Christmas carols.

During medieval days, the word carol meant "dancing in a ring while singing." Merrymakers used these ring-dances to celebrate most festivals. By the fifteenth century, the word carol was used mainly to describe joyful Christmas songs.

Most of the early carols were made up by simple folk. They sang new Christmas words to old dance tunes and folk music. Parents passed the carols down to their children. Minstrels sang them in their travels. Christmas carols came from many countries, passed along by word of mouth.

Some were gentle lullabies, like this Polish carol:

> Hush, hush, the Babe doth rest—
> Stilled is His weeping.
> Like a small bird
> By His Mother He's sleeping.
> Lullaby, Jesus Child.

41

Other carols told about Christmas customs. Celebrations in France centered around the crèche. Grownups and children paraded from house to house, singing carols, called noëls, around their crèches. Noël, or nowel, also means news.

Bring a torch, Jeannette, Isabella!
Bring a torch, to the cradle run!
It is Jesus, good folk of the village;
Christ is born and Mary's calling.
Ah! ah! Beautiful is the Mother!
Ah! ah! Beautiful is her Son!

People made up carols about the Holy Family, the shepherds, the Wise Men, and the Star. Most of the early carols were sung by strolling carolers outdoors.

"Here we come a-wassailing," carolers announced their coming. The expression of good wishes, or "wassailing" had become another word for caroling. Lighted windows signaled the singers to stop. Sometimes the carolers were gay troops of children, singing for treats. Caroling brought good fortune to homes, people said.

Musicians sometimes strolled with the carolers. Drums, oboes, clarinets, fiddles, and handbells were popular instruments. Expert handbell ringers added much beauty to carol singing.

Bells, like carols, were called "Voices of Christmas." Bells then were used to announce news as well as to make music. Church bells tolled slowly for an hour before midnight on Christmas Eve. Then they rang out joyfully as if to say, "Rejoice! Christmas has come." The melody of church bells and handbells filled the air during the Christmas season.

The first printed book of carols appeared in 1521. Since then, many old carols have been collected and printed. Poets and songwriters added others. The stories behind some of these new carols are as beautiful as the songs. Here is one of them:

In the village of Oberndorf, Austria, lived two friends. One was Father Josef

Mohr, the young village priest. The other was Franz Gruber, the schoolteacher. The two friends often sang together, while Gruber played the church organ or his guitar.

On Christmas Eve, 1818, Father Mohr went to bless the newborn babe of a peasant mother. It was dark as he walked

home through the forest. Trees stood in snowy silence under shining stars. The priest thought of the Holy Night when the Star shone, angels sang, and a Babe was born in Bethlehem. He hurried home and put his feelings into a poem.

His friend, Gruber, quickly set the words to music. "It was easy," he said. "Your words sang themselves."

The two friends sang the new song in church that Christmas Day. The organ was broken, so Gruber played his guitar. Many listeners called the carol "Song from Heaven." Later, it became famous as the carol "Silent Night! Holy Night!"

9.   Christmas Gift-Bringers

And when they had opened their treasures,
They presented unto Him gifts;
Gold, and frankincense, and myrrh.
          —The Gospel According to St. Matthew

The first Christmas gifts were given to the Christ Child. The Wise Men were the gift-bringers. The gold, frankincense, and myrrh honored His birth.

In time, Christ's birthday became a gift day for most children in Europe. The gift-bringers have had many forms through the years. Most of them come secretly at night.

They leave treats for good children and reminders of punishment for naughty ones.

Saint Nicholas was the best known gift-bringer in medieval times. A real St. Nicholas lived in the fourth century. He was a Bishop of Myra, in the land now called Turkey, and was famous for his generosity and his love for children. He used all of his money to give gifts to children and to poor people. His gifts were given in secret. Whenever anyone received a surprise gift, he would say, "Oh, St. Nicholas gave it."

Many legends arose about the generosity of St. Nicholas. These spread over Europe during the Middle Ages. December 6 was made his feast day, or "birthday." It was also made the gift day for children in many countries.

St. Nicholas represented the spirit of Christmas giving. He was pictured dressed as a Bishop, riding a white horse or donkey.

The Lapps pictured him driving through snow in a sleigh drawn by reindeer.

The St. Nicholas customs were especially popular in Holland. Dutch children called the saint, *Sinter Klaas*. On the eve of December 6, children placed their shoes or stockings by fireplaces. They left hay, carrots, or sugar for St. Nicholas' horse or donkey. These would be gone next morning. In their places, children found surprise gifts. Naughty children found switches as reminders to be good.

"St. Nicholas brought the gifts down the chimney," children were told. This idea came partly from a St. Nicholas legend. Once there were three sisters who were very poor. St. Nicholas climbed secretly to their housetop and dropped three bags of money down the chimney. The bags rolled into shoes left by the fireplace to dry.

The custom also may have come from a Scandinavian myth. Hertha was the Scandinavian goddess of hearth and home fires. Every winter Hertha came through fires or down fireplaces, bringing happiness and good fortune.

The 1500's brought the beginning of Protestant churches. Many people now changed their gift day to Christ's birthday. Gift-bringers left surprises on Christmas Eve, while children slept.

The spirit of St. Nicholas took the form of a "Christmas Man" in several countries. Children called him Father Christmas in

England, and *Père Noël* in France. He was often pictured as tall and stately, with a long white beard.

The Christ Child was adopted as another symbol of Christmas giving. The German name for the Christ Child is *Christkind.* In French it is *Petit Noël,* in Spanish, *Niño Jesús,* and in Italian, *Gesù Bambino.*

Gift-bringers in Scandinavian countries are elf-men with long white whiskers. They are called *Jule-Nisser* in Norway and in Denmark, and *Jule-Tomtar* in Sweden. On Christmas Eve, children set out bowls of rice pudding, a favorite dessert. The wee gift-bringers leave presents as thanks.

Children in Spain think of the Wise Men as gift-bringers. Gifts are received on January 6, the date the Wise Men gave gifts to the Christ Child.

Children in Italy also receive gifts on Epiphany. They have a lady gift-bringer, Befana. The name comes from "Epiphany."

51

The Wise Men begged Befana to take gifts to the Holy Babe, legends say. "I'll go tomorrow," she told them. She went, but never found Bethlehem. So each Christmas Befana leaves gifts for all children, hoping that one will be Jesus.

There is a similar legend told about Babushka, the old Russian gift-bringer. "Babushka" means grandmother.

The names and forms of gift-bringers have changed in most countries as centuries

passed. But the spirit remains the same. They bring their gifts of love to honor the birthday of Christ.

In America, several gift-bringers gradually became one. Dutch settlers brought their *Sinter Klaas.* English settlers brought Father Christmas, and German settlers brought *Christkind.* All of these gift-bringers combined into a new Christmas visitor. He is the kind, jolly, roly-poly, rosy-cheeked man called Santa Claus.

10.   A New Kind
of Christmas

"No Christmas! No Christmas!"
Town criers clanged handbells and shouted this warning in England. The Puritans controlled the English government in the 1640's. This stern religious group felt that Christmas had grown too gay and rowdy. So they passed laws to stop all festivity on religious holidays.

The laws were strict. All shops and markets had to stay open on Christmas Day. There could be no carol singing, Yule feasts, or merrymaking. December 25 was treated as a common work day. Anyone caught celebrating could be punished.

People celebrated secretly in their homes, and luckily, the laws did not last long. King Charles II revived public celebrations in the 1660's. "Bring your customs out of hiding," the people were told.

A new kind of Christmas began then. Celebrations were merry, but much simpler for rich and poor alike. Christmas became a time for families to get together. Poor people no longer went to castles for handouts. Peasants had gained more rights, and had a bit more money to spend. Peasants, middle class and noblemen held feasts in their own homes. This was true in other countries of Europe, as well as in England.

The roast goose was the meat of honor, and the plum pudding was the favorite dessert. What fun families had making their pudding! Everyone took turns stirring it. Everyone made a wish as he stirred. Before the pudding was served, a sprig of holly was stuck on top. Brandy poured on the pudding was lighted. Cheers rang out when the pudding reached the table.

Such feasts were especially popular in England. Charles Dickens described one in his story, *A Christmas Carol,* published in 1843. Dickens was one of the first authors to write about the way ordinary people celebrated Christmas. His famous Christmas stories helped to spread these customs, and made them more popular. *A Christmas Carol* is still read every year, in homes and schoolrooms. The story reminds everyone

of the true spirit of Christmas—love and kindness to all.

Christmas customs were flourishing all over Europe during the 1800's. A new idea had helped to make Christmas the children's favorite festival. That was the Christmas tree. The Germans were the first to center family celebrations around Christmas trees. Their trees in the 1500's were decorated with apples and sweets, but had no lights. Candles were placed on Christmas pyramids.

Pyramids were made by fastening shelves to a stand. Each shelf was smaller than the one beneath it, forming a pyramid shape. Shelves could be round, square, triangular, or rectangular. They were gaily decorated with evergreens, ornaments, and candles.

Later, German families began placing the candles on their trees instead. It is said that Martin Luther, the sixteenth century German church leader, began this custom.

One starry Christmas Eve, Luther walked through a snow-covered forest. Twinkling stars seemed to light up the evergreen trees. Luther longed to share the beauty with his children. He took a fir tree home and trimmed it with candles to stand for the stars. His children were overjoyed by the lovely sight.

Word of the Luthers' tree spread and by the early seventeenth century other German children shared this joy. On Christmas Eve, families lit the candles on their trees and sang carols around them. A favorite song of the Christmas season came to be "O Tannenbaum," the German for "O Christmas Tree."

> O Christmas tree, O Christmas tree,
> With happiness we greet you.
> When decked with candles once a year
> You fill our hearts with Yuletide cheer,
> O Christmas tree, O Christmas tree,
> With happiness we greet you.

The Christmas tree custom spread slowly, but surely. It reached most European countries in the nineteenth century. Then a German prince helped make it popular in England. When Prince Albert of Germany married Queen Victoria of England, he set up a Christmas tree in Windsor Castle. After that, the fashion spread rapidly.

The fir was the favorite tree. Pine, spruce, yew, and cedar also grew popular. Early tree decorations were homemade—colored paper, berries, straw, feathers, cookies, and trinkets. Germans often covered apples with colored paper. This led to the idea of colored balls.

The first colored glass ornaments were made by German peasants in their cottages. As Christmas trees grew more popular, tree ornaments developed into a big industry.

German settlers brought their Christmas tree customs to America. Here they joined customs brought from other parts of Europe. By the 1860's, Christmas celebrations were popular all over America.

Interestingly enough, America gave new Christmas traditions to Europe. One was the turkey. Sixteenth century explorers found wild turkeys in Mexico, and took some to Europe. They were tamed, raised, and later enjoyed as a Christmas meat.

11. Merry Christmas to You

One of the newest Christmas customs grew to be one of the most popular. This is the sending of Christmas greeting cards.

Schoolboys in England probably sent the first Christmas cards. In the early 1800's, English students sent out "Christmas Pieces" just before the holidays. Christmas Pieces were greetings to their parents, written on decorated sheets of paper. Students tried to show off their progress in composition and penmanship.

True Christmas cards came into being in the 1840's. An Englishman, Sir Henry Cole, had 1,000 cards printed and sold. These cards were hand-painted by an artist, John C. Horsley. They were made of stiff cardboard, about the size of a modern postcard.

Soon other Englishmen began making personal cards to send to friends. These cards were costly, though. Only people with a great deal of money could afford to send them.

By the 1860's, printing companies began to make and sell Christmas cards. Many of these first cards were works of art. Card companies held contests to find the best designs. One contest prize was $10,000. The most popular artists then illustrated Christmas cards.

Several artists found fame because of their card designs. Kate Greenaway was one of them. Her Christmas cards led to her career as an illustrator of children's books. Her illustrated books of verses are still popular.

The Christmas card custom was widespread in Europe and America by the 1870's. New printing processes and cheaper postage helped. Christmas cards proved to be a wonderful way of saying "Merry Christmas" to anyone, anywhere.

The Christmas story never ends. Each century adds new customs, legends, songs, and symbols. All of these serve to carry the message of Christmas. This message remains the same as it was told on the first Christmas: GLORY, PEACE, GOOD WILL.

We wish you a Merry Christmas,
We wish you a Merry Christmas,
We wish you a Merry Christmas,
And a Happy New Year.
Good tidings we bring
To you and your kin;
Good tidings for Christmas
And a Happy New Year!
—*Old English or Scottish Carol*